Barra is a beautiful island.
Visitors come here for
holidays.
They walk in the hills and
enjoy the sandy beaches.

Visitors to Barra can stay
in this new hotel.

The weather is wet and windy
on Barra. There are very few
trees or crops.
Potatoes can be grown on
patches of fertile soil near the sea.

Many people who live on Barra
are farmers.
They keep cattle and sheep.

SSI

Barra

Look at the map of Scotland. There are lots of islands in the sea. One of the islands is called Barra.

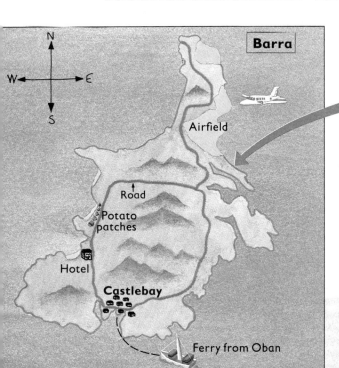

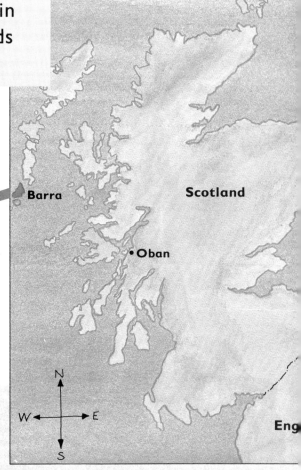

Look at the map of Barra. Castlebay is in the south. What is in the north?

Barra is a small island. Most people on Barra live in the village called Castlebay.

Some people earn their living
by fishing.
The lorry in this picture is
taking fish from the boats
to Castlebay.

Sheep, cattle and fish are sold
at markets on the mainland.
They are taken by ferry
from Castlebay.
You can see the fish lorry
on this ferry.

Most people travel
to and from Barra
by ferry. It takes
five hours to sail
from Barra to Obar
Oban is a town
on the mainland.

Some people travel to Barra by plane.
This flat sandy beach is also
an airfield. Small planes land and
take off here.

Oban railway station is near the harbour.

People can travel to Oban by train, then they catch the ferry to Barra and other Scottish islands.

This picture of Oban shows the town and the harbour.

Tristan da Cunha

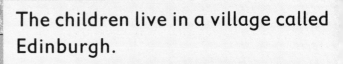

These children live on one of the most remote islands in the world. The island is called Tristan da Cunha.

The children live in a village called Edinburgh.

Edinburgh is the only village on the island.
The village is on flat land next to the sea.
This is the only large area of flat land on Tristan.

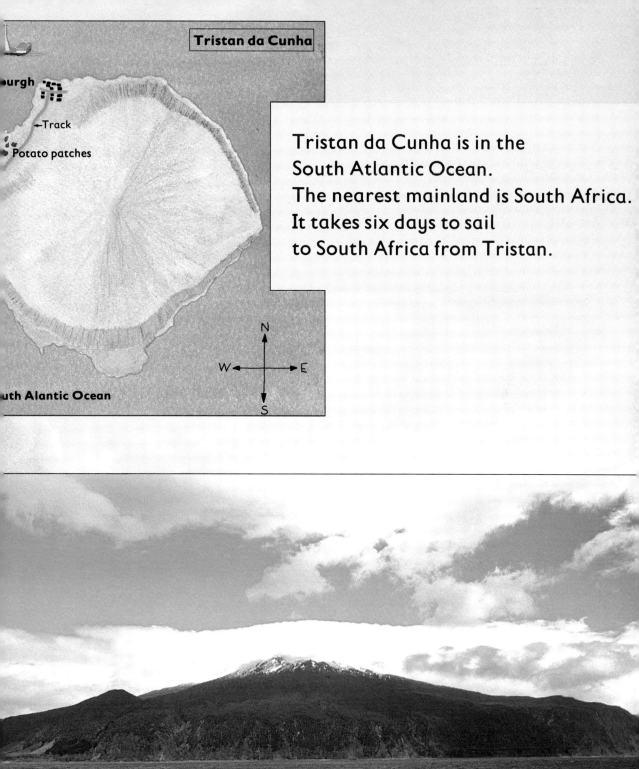

Tristan da Cunha

urgh

←Track

Potato patches

uth Alantic Ocean

N
W ← → E
S

Tristan da Cunha is in the
South Atlantic Ocean.
The nearest mainland is South Africa.
It takes six days to sail
to South Africa from Tristan.

The people of Tristan built their houses from stone. The oldest houses had thatched roofs like this one. There are three thatched houses left on the island.

Houses have iron or asbestos roofs today. Many of the older houses have been made bigger.

The islanders keep sheep and cows.
What do they get from these animals?

he islanders grow most of their own food.
otatoes are the main crop on Tristan.
hey grow well in the cool, wet weather.

The people of Tristan earn most of their money from fishing. These fishing boats are sheltering in the harbour. It is often too windy for them to go out.

The islanders catch and sell shellfish called crawfish.

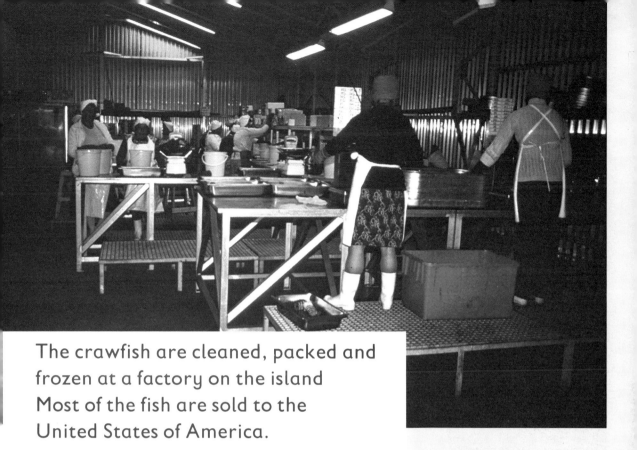

The crawfish are cleaned, packed and
frozen at a factory on the island
Most of the fish are sold to the
United States of America.

This ship is in Cape Town harbour
in South Africa.
It takes fish away from Tristan and
brings mail and other goods to the island.

The island of Tristan is a volcano. In 1961, disaster struck. Red-hot lava poured out of the ground near the village.

The islanders were in great danger and had to leave Tristan quickly. They were rescued by a passing ship.

£2 EℝR
TRISTAN DA CUNHA

The ship took the islanders to England, where they lived for nearly three years. When the volcano had stopped erupting most people returned home.

The lava had covered land near the village, but the houses were safe.

The islanders were very glad to be home again.

Dominica

Dominica is a tropical island in the Caribbean Sea.

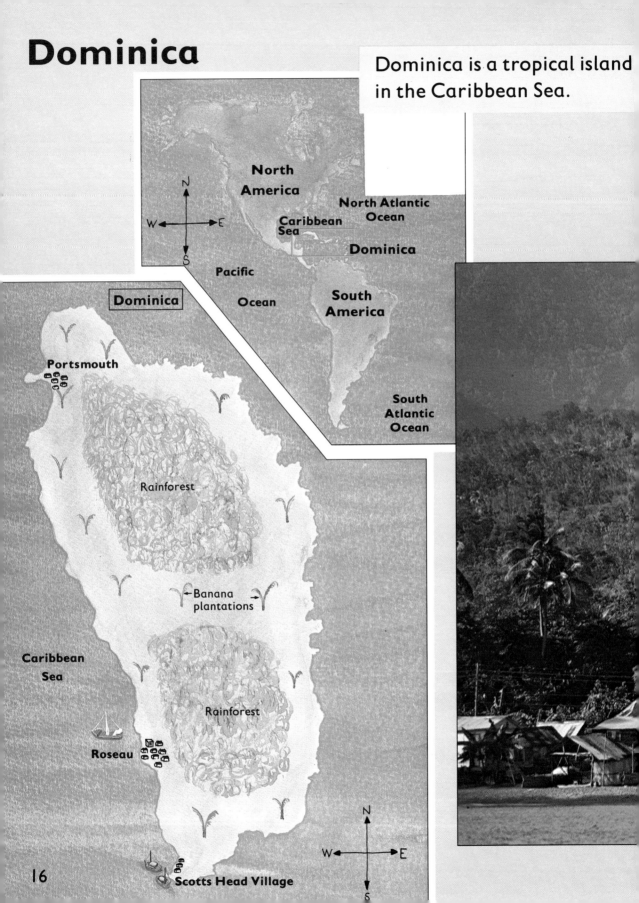

North America

North Atlantic Ocean

Caribbean Sea

Dominica

Pacific Ocean

South America

South Atlantic Ocean

N
W   E
S

Dominica

Portsmouth

Rainforest

Banana plantations

Caribbean Sea

Rainforest

Roseau

N
W   E
S

Scotts Head Village

It is hot and rainy
on Dominica.
Thick rainforest grows
on the mountains in the
middle of the island.

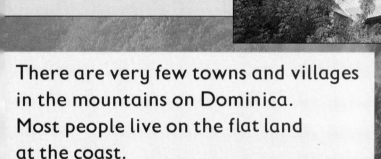

There are very few towns and villages
in the mountains on Dominica.
Most people live on the flat land
at the coast.

This fishing village is called Scotts Head. Look for the fishing boats on the beach.

Small fishing boats stay close to the shore.

Further out to sea, the weather can be stormy and dangerous.

The fishermen will sell most of these sprats in local markets. They will take some fish home to their families.

Bananas are the most important crop on the island. They grow well in hot, rainy places.

Some banana farmers live in small houses like this one. It is made of wood and corrugated iron.

The bananas grow in large bunches. Each banana gets fatter as it grows.

Bananas are cut when they
are still green.
They are packed into boxes
as soon as they are picked.

The boxes of bananas are loaded
into small boats, then taken to a ship.

Most of the bananas which grow on
Dominica are sold in Britain.

Many tourists visit Dominica. Most of them travel to the island on cruise ships like this one.

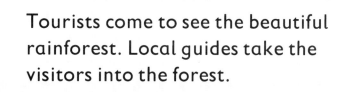

Tourists come to see the beautiful rainforest. Local guides take the visitors into the forest.

Some tourists travel into the forest by boat.

The biggest town on Dominica is called Roseau.

This is one of the main shopping streets in Roseau.

Roads link the town with the small villages on the island. People usually travel into Roseau by bus.

On Saturdays there is a market in Roseau. Here, people buy and sell flowers, fruit , vegetables and fish. Local people and visitors come to shop at the market.

Once a year there is a carnival in Roseau. Children and adults dress up for the carnival and they all walk through the streets. Everyone comes out to watch the parade.

Index